Charley's Cha

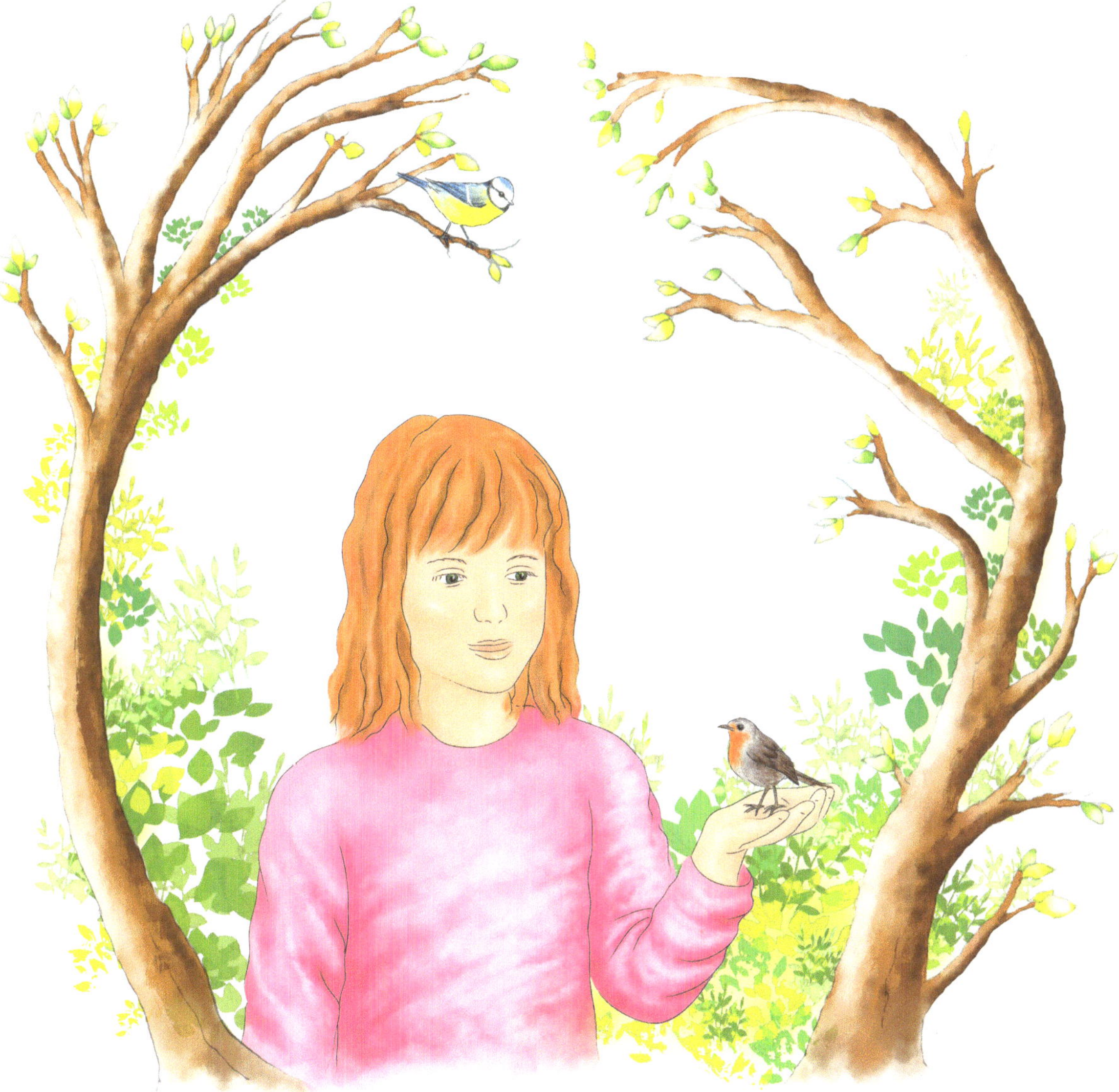

**Author and Illustrator
Emma J Richardson**

ISBN 978-1-0684176-0-3

Copyright © Emma J Richardson 2025.
First edition, published 2025.
All rights reserved.

No part of this book may be reproduced, transmitted, or stored in a retreival system, without prior permission of Emma J Richardson.
All characters, places and events are fictitious and imagined by the author. Any resemblance to actual people, places or events is purely coincidental.

Visit the author's website at www.emmajrichardson.co.uk

This is Charley.
She is 7 years old.

Charley loves wildlife. She enjoys going to the park and feeding the ducks.

She is never happier than when she is watching and drawing birds in the garden.

There's one more thing to tell you about Charley.

Charley is autistic. For her this means...

...she doesn't like crowds...

...some noises can be almost painful...

...and she finds it hard to make new friends.

However, when something really interests her, she likes to learn as much as she can about it. She can become quite an expert!

At school, Charley's favourite subjects are art and English.

But she doesn't like maths very much!

Charley's favourite part of the day is break time, when she sits somewhere quiet with her friend Alex and chats.

Charley copes well with the difficulties of being autistic and is happy. But things were about to change.

One night, at home, her mum said, "Charley, come downstairs please, I want to talk to you."

Her mum said, "I've got exciting news, we are going to move to a new house in a new town."

Charley's mind started racing with all the things she would miss.

Leading up to the move, Charley still felt worried so her mum took her to the park to feed the ducks.

She saw a group of barnacle geese, flying north for the spring. She thought, "If geese can move home, maybe I can."

When the time eventually came to move, Charley's mum was very excited.

Charley pretended to be happy but inside she was very anxious.

The move also meant that Charley had to attend a new school.

Charley went to her new school, which was huge and noisy.

It was quite overwhelming.

When she tried to block out the noise, other children didn't understand.

"Put your thinking caps on and work together as a table," said the teacher.

When Charley came home from school she looked very unhappy. "I didn't enjoy school one bit!" she said.

Charley's mum explained, "A lot of children feel worried when moving to a new home or school, being autistic can make you more anxious than most."

"Don't worry, just give it some time," said her mum.

Charley said, "I HATE this new house,
I HATE the new school,
I HATE being autistic!"

Charley's mum persuaded her to give her new school another try, but Charley was still nervous.

The first lesson was maths. "Even worse," Charley thought. She looked out of the window and saw something interesting.

"What are you looking at Charley?" asked the teacher.

"Oops," thought Charley. She explained, "I was watching the blackbirds outside, they are making a nest."

"They'll soon be laying three to five blue-green eggs."

"Really?" asked the teacher. "Do you know anything else about birds?"

"Lots," said Charley and she talked about all the birds she knew.

At break time, Ella, a girl from Charley's class, approached her. "How do you know so much about birds?" she asked.

"I'm just interested," replied Charley, "but I'm also autistic, maybe that helps?"

"What does autistic mean?" asked Ella. "My brain works differently," replied Charley, "sometimes it makes me worried, and sometimes it distracts me. But when I'm interested in something it makes me excited and keen to know more."

"I'd like to know more about birds," said Ella, "can you show me?"

When Charley came home from school that evening, her mum asked, "Was school any better today?"

"Much better," said Charley, "I told the class about birds and I made a new friend."

"She wants me to teach her about birds," said Charley.

Then Charley had an idea.

The next day Charley saw Ella at school. "Do you want to come round to my house to watch the birds?" Charley asked. "Yes please," replied Ella.

Charley feels much happier now, with her birds, her garden, her friend, and being autistic. It all makes Charley who she is.

www.ingramcontent.com/pod-product-compliance
Ingram Content Group UK Ltd.
Pitfield, Milton Keynes, MK11 3LW, UK
UKHW021734090425
5401UKWH00022B/128